KT-450-764

Scary Spiders

Lynn Huggins-Cooper

W
FRANKLIN WATTS

9030 00000 2846 6

This edition 2008/2009

Franklin Watts
338 Euston Road
London NW1 3BH

Franklin Watts Australia
Hachette Children's Books
Level 17/207 Kent Street,
Sydney NSW 2000

Copyright © Franklin Watts 2005

LONDON BOROUGH OF WANDSWORTH	
9030 00000 2846 6	
Askews	07-May-2009
C595.44153 HUGG	£6.99
	WWX0004505/0016

Editor: Jennifer Schofield
Art director and Jacket designer: Peter Scoulding
Designer: Jay Young
Picture researcher: Diana Morris

Acknowledgements:
Carol Buchanan/Photographers Direct: 26. Densey Clyne/ANTPhoto.com:
29. Gerry Ellis/FLPA: front cover cl, 20. Ken Griffiths/ANTPhoto.com: 28.
Daniel Heuclin/NHPA: 7, 11. Andrés Morya Hinojosa/Photographers Direct:
10. Wernher Krutein/Photovault: 5, 22. Norman Larsen: 24, 25. Rod Preston-
Mafham/Premaphotos: 9, 15, 16, 18. Edward L Manigault/Clemson University
Donated Collection/Insect Images.org: 17. Chris Mattison/Photographers
Direct: 8. Buddy Mays/Photographers Direct: 6. Jurgen Otto/ANTPhoto.com:
27. Kjell Sandved/Ecoscene: front cover bl, 1. Francesco Tomaselli/Natural Visions:
12, 14, 23. Francesco Tomaselli/tips images: 21. Alan Towse/Ecoscene: front cover
r, 4. Richard Uhlhorn/Photographers Direct: 19. Visual Unlimited/Mediscan: 13.

Every attempt has been made to clear copyright.
Should there be any inadvertent omission please
apply to the publisher for rectification.

A CIP catalogue record for this book
is available from the British Library.

ISBN: 978 0 7496 8317 7
Dewey Classification: 595.4'4

Printed in China

Franklin Watts is a division of Hachette Children's Books, an Hachette UK company.
www.hachettelivre.co.uk

Contents

Scary spiders

Scuttling across the kitchen wall, sitting in the bathtub or spinning webs across the garden path – there is no doubt about it, spiders can be very spooky! But are these scary animals as bad as they seem?

Spider facts

Spiders belong to a group of animals called arachnids. Scorpions, ticks and mites are also arachnids. All arachnids have eight legs and their bodies are divided into two parts. Arachnids do not have wings or antennae to feel their way.

Many spiders spin silk. They use it to make webs or traps for prey. They also use it to travel from place to place, just like the superhero Spiderman.

Friend or foe?

There are more than 35,000 different species of spider. Although many people are terrified of these web-spinning beasts, not all spiders are dangerous. Spiders hunt and kill harmful flies and bugs that can cause deadly diseases.

However, some spiders can give a poisonous – and even fatal – bite. So, can you tell whether a spider is a friend or foe? Read on to find out – it just might save your life one day!

Beastly black widows

Black widows are found in warm, tropical regions. They also live in the deserts of southwestern USA. If you disturb one of these spiders, it could give you a nasty bite.

Vital statistics

Female black widows are about 2–2.5 centimetres long and weigh only a gram. Male black widows are about half the size of the females. Black widows build their webs close to the ground. Their webs can be up to 30 centimetres wide.

Fact!

Black widows are also called hourglass spiders because of the red shape on the female's abdomen.

How they kill

Male black widows are harmless but the females are poisonous. The spiders are shy and they hide in their webs during the day. At night, they hang belly-up in the middle of their webs. They wait for insects and small reptiles or mammals to be caught in the web. The spiders then inject the prey with venom and digestive juices. This stops the prey from moving and kills it. The animal's flesh becomes mushy so that the spider can suck it up.

Encounters with people

Black widows spin their webs in log piles, under stones and in the burrows of small animals. The spiders are also found in sheds, garages and even in outside toilets.

Although black widows may come into contact with people, they do not attack unless they are disturbed – for example, if a person brushes against their web or if the spider is trapped in clothing.

More about black widows

When black widows bite

A black widow bite looks like a target – there is a red ring around a pale area. The bite is not very painful for humans, but it can cause other problems, most often in young children and old or ill adults. These problems include sweating, finding it hard to breathe, vomiting, headaches, terrible stomach pain and aching muscles. However, less than one per cent of the people bitten by black widows die. This is because there is an antivenin to fight the spider's poison.

Fact!

Black widows have a row of bristles on each back leg. They use these to wrap silk around their prey.

Survival

Black widows are not endangered. Their conservation is important because doctors are studying their venom. They hope that the venom can be used for medicine to make blood thinner. When blood is thin, it pumps around the body more easily. This helps to stop people from having heart attacks.

Baby black widows

Female black widows lay between 250 and 700 eggs in an egg sac. Each year, they may spin four to nine sacs. The young spiders hatch after 14 to 30 days. Only one to 12 babies survive – the rest are eaten by their brothers and sisters.

When black widows are born, they are a cream colour. They become darker each time they moult. The baby spiders leave the egg sac by spinning long silk threads to catch the wind. The baby spiders float away like balloons.

Shy brown recluses

Brown recluses are found in central and southern parts of the USA. They are called recluses because they are shy and like to hide in dark places.

Sometimes brown recluses are also called fiddlebacks or violin spiders because they have a fiddle (violin) shape on their head and back.

Fact!

Recluse spiders are easy to trap. An American researcher caught 40 spiders in 75 minutes!

Vital statistics

Brown recluses are about 1 centimetre long. The adult males have smaller bodies than the females, but their legs are longer. These spiders have six eyes rather than eight like most other spiders.

How they kill

Brown recluses are nocturnal. During the day, they sleep in their messy webs. But at night, they look for food. Male recluses are scavengers and they eat carrion – the rotting flesh of animals. Females attack prey, such as bugs, with their fangs and inject it with venom.

Baby brown recluses

Female brown recluse spiders lay about 50 eggs in a cream-coloured egg sac. Like black widows, they can spin several egg sacs each year. Baby spiders come out of the sacs after about a month. It takes a year before they are fully grown.

Encounters with people

Although recluses are shy spiders, if people disturb them, they may bite. They spin their webs in dark places such as attics, cellars and under verandahs. Often they can be found in sheds, barns and garages.

People can keep brown recluse spiders away from their homes by making sure their attics and basements are clean and tidy. Areas where the spiders could hide, such as cracks in walls, should also be sealed off.

More about recluses

Survival

Brown recluse spiders are not an endangered species. In fact, they can be a pest. Large numbers of them can take over or infest homes. When this happens, a pest control expert has to be called in to kill the deadly spiders.

Fact!

Brown recluses can survive for six months without food or water.

When brown recluses bite

Recluses are not aggressive. They bite people only when they are disturbed, for example if someone accidentally touches them or their web. Spookily, a recluse may crawl into a bed and bite the person in it as he or she rolls over!

Recluse spider bites kill the skin around them. The bites swell and can become a rotting and infected hole. Brown recluse spider bites can kill young children and elderly people, but this is very unusual.

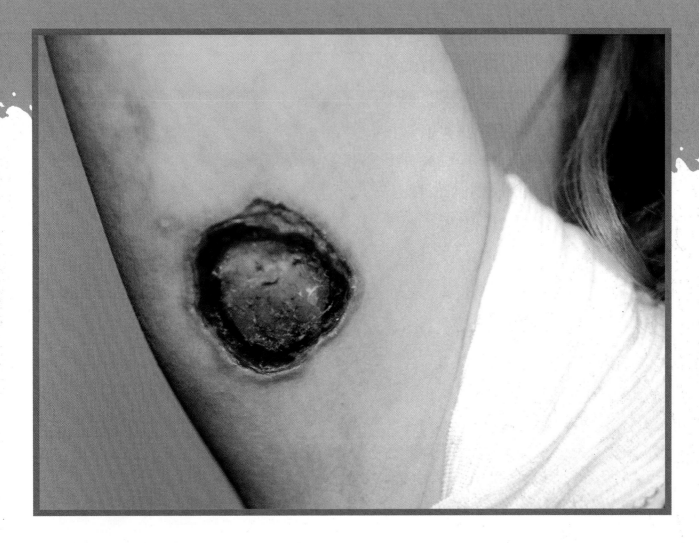

Real-life story

In 2002, Dale Losher from Illinois, USA, was bitten by a brown recluse. He was bitten when he picked up a duvet from the floor to put on his bed. Unfortunately, a recluse spider was hiding in the quilt. Dale's leg was red and stinging, so he went straight to the doctor. He needed four operations to take away dead skin from the 13-centimetre hole in his leg.

Leggy yellow sacs

Yellow sac spiders are one of the most common types of house spider in North America. They are a yellow-green colour and have dark-coloured fangs. Yellow sac spiders move around the country, often by accident in boxes of fruit such as grapes.

Encounters with people

Like many other spiders, yellow sacs will not attack humans unless they are disturbed or feel threatened. As they are found in places where people live, it is easy to disturb them accidentally. When the spiders are disturbed, they drop to the ground to run away – so you would not want to be standing underneath a yellow sac!

Vital statistics

Yellow sac spiders are quite small – their bodies measure about 1 centimetre long. However, these pale yellow spiders have long legs that can measure 19 centimetres.

Baby yellow sac spiders

Female yellow sac spiders spin an egg sac. They hide the sac in leaves or stones. They lay between 30 and 48 eggs in each sac. The females guard the eggs until the baby spiders hatch.

How they kill

Yellow sacs use their first pair of legs as feelers while they search amongst plants for prey. Once they have found a victim, the spiders attack their prey with a deadly bite.

When yellow sacs bite

A yellow sac bite is not very painful to people – it feels like a bee sting. However, not long after the bite, victims begin to feel dizzy. They may also have a fever and feel like vomiting. Sometimes, the skin around a bite becomes infected and open sores can form. These sores look like a 'flesh-eating' disease.

Fact!

Brown recluses are often blamed for yellow sac bites because their bites are similar.

Horrible hobo spiders

Hobo spiders are found in the USA, western Canada and western Europe. These deadly spiders were brought from Europe to the USA in the 1930s by ships carrying goods. Hobo spiders live mainly in the countryside, in holes, cracks in the ground and in open fields.

Vital statistics

Hobo spiders measure between 1.2 and 1.8 centimetres long. Their leg-span can reach to about 3 centimetres. Like many spiders, they are a brown-grey colour. It can be difficult to tell the difference between the hobo spider and its harmless relative, the giant house spider (below).

How they kill

Hobo spiders spin flat, funnel-shaped webs. The webs are not very sticky, but they have threads to trip and trap prey. The spiders prey mainly on bugs. When a bug tries to get free from the trip-lines, the spiders follow the movement to find it. Once the prey is found, the spiders rush out, grab the prey and take it back to the wider part of the web to eat it.

More about hobos

Survival

Hobo spiders are very common. In the USA, there are so many of them that they need to be killed with pesticides. These do not always work. Sometimes they kill other harmless spiders, too. Dogs, birds and especially house cats also kill the spiders.

Baby hobo spiders

Female hobo spiders produce between one and four silken egg sacs. The sacs are usually attached to the undersides of rocks or wood. Each egg sac can hold up to 100 eggs. The young hobo spiders hatch from the eggs after eight or nine months.

When hobos attack

Usually, hobo spiders will bite people only when they are trapped, perhaps in clothing or bedding. In about half the hobo bites on people, no poison is injected.

When the spiders do inject poison, the wound feels like a mosquito bite. After 24 hours, a blister forms in the centre of the bite. This can break open and leave an oozing sore which takes a long time to heal.

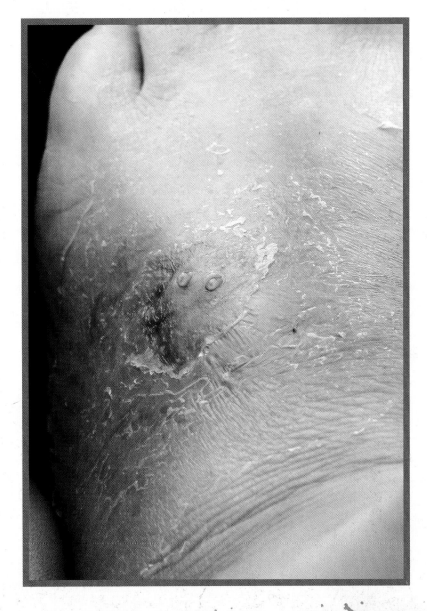

Real-life story

In 2000 in Seattle, USA, Gerardo Chavez was bitten by a hobo spider while he was sleeping. The spider may have been trapped in Gerardo's bedding and bit him to defend itself.

Five days later, the 19-year-old's bite was so infected he was taken to hospital. Both of Gerardo's legs had to be cut off above the knee. He also needed a heart operation to stay alive.

Hairy tarantulas

These huge spiders are creatures from nightmares and horror films, with their fat, hairy bodies and long wiry legs. There are more than 800 different species of tarantula. They are found throughout the world in hot countries. Tarantulas live in abandoned burrows, under rocks and logs, and among crops, such as pineapples.

Vital statistics

Most tarantulas are black or brown but some are more colourful. For example, Mexican red-legged tarantulas (left) have red markings on their legs.

The tarantula family also includes some of the biggest spiders in the world. Goliath tarantulas from South America have a body of up to 13 centimetres long. Their legs can stretch to an amazing 30 centimetres – the same length as a school ruler!

Survival

Tarantulas are not endangered. However, their numbers are dropping as their habitat is being cleared for farming and building. Many are also caught as pets.

How they kill

Tarantulas feed on animals such as grasshoppers, crickets, other spiders and small lizards. These hairy beasts are unlike most spiders because they do not spin webs. Instead, they chase and hunt their prey.

When the spiders have caught their victim, they use their fangs to inject deadly poison. They grind the prey into a ball and turn it into a mushy liquid. When the prey is really runny, they suck up the juice.

More about tarantulas

Encounters with people

Tarantulas look scary but they are not aggressive. Their bite is painful but not fatal.

When they are disturbed, tarantulas throw fine hairs towards the danger. If these hairs enter people's skin, they cause a rash. The rash can lead to fainting and breathing problems.

If handled carefully, these hairy spiders can be quite safe. Many people choose to keep them as pets.

Fact!
Tarantulas warn off predators by rubbing their jaws and front legs against each other to make a noise.

Baby tarantulas

Female tarantulas lay eggs in silk egg sacs. They seal the sacs after laying between 500 and 1,000 eggs. The females then stand guard, protecting the sacs until the eggs hatch. This takes about six to nine weeks. Tarantulas can live for an incredibly long time – between 25 and 40 years.

Six-eyed sand spiders

Six-eyed sand spiders have lived on Earth for millions of years. They are found in southwest Africa, usually in the desert and dry areas.

These spiders live on sand dunes where they bury themselves in the sand. They also hide under rocks and near insect holes.

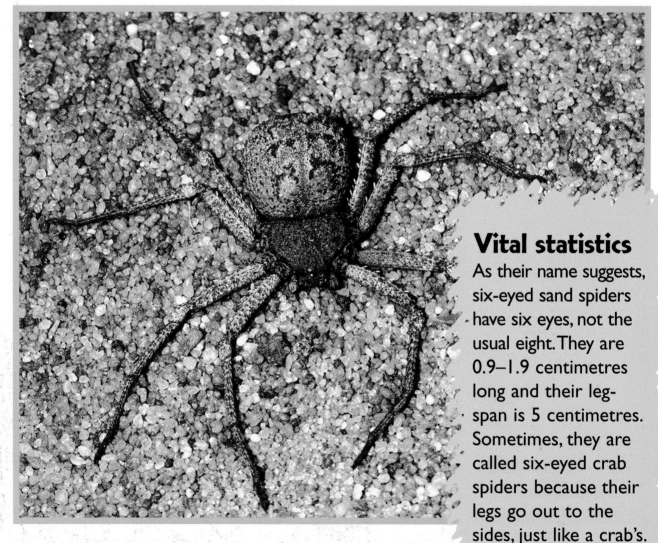

Vital statistics

As their name suggests, six-eyed sand spiders have six eyes, not the usual eight. They are 0.9–1.9 centimetres long and their leg-span is 5 centimetres. Sometimes, they are called six-eyed crab spiders because their legs go out to the sides, just like a crab's.

Encounters with people

The venom of the six-eyed sand spider can cause bleeding inside the body. If this is not treated, it can kill a person. Luckily, bites are rare because the spiders live in deserts, far away from people.

Baby six-eyed sand spiders

The female spiders make a cup-shaped egg sac from sand and silk. The sac is buried in sand. Once the eggs hatch, the baby spiders come crawling out from under the ground.

Fact!
Six-eyed sand spiders can live for up to a year without food or water.

How they kill

Six-eyed sand spiders are sly killers. They scoop out sand to make a pit, crawl into the pit and cover themselves with sand. They wait in their pit for prey. As the prey walks across the pit, they leap up and grab the insects with their front legs.

Vicious red-backs

Red-back spiders are found in most parts of Australia and in some southeast Asian countries. They live in towns and cities, near people.

Red-backs are often seen crawling about in rubbish bins, on patios and, very scarily, under the seats of outdoor toilets.

Fact!
A red-back bite becomes wet with sweat but the skin on the rest of the body stays dry.

Vital statistics

Red-back spiders are easy to recognise. They are black with a red, pink or even grey mark on their back. Red-backs also have long, skinny legs.

Female red-backs measure about 1 centimetre long. Males are much smaller – their bodies are less than 0.5 centimetres long.

How they kill

Red-back spiders eat insects, other spiders and small lizards. The females make funnel-shaped webs with sticky 'catching lines' running from the web to the ground. When prey is caught in the lines, the spider scuttles down the catching lines. It bites the prey and wraps it in silk before eating it.

Encounters with people

Each year, hundreds of Australians are bitten by red-back spiders. Before an antivenin was made to combat the poison of the red-back, people who were bitten by red-backs would die. Since the antivenin was made in 1956, no one has died from the bite of a red-back spider.

Baby red-backs

Female red-backs spin up to eight light yellow egg sacs. Each sac may hold as many as 300 eggs. In warm weather, the tiny baby spiders hatch after about two weeks. Just like baby black widows, the young spiders balloon away on silk strands.

When red-backs bite

At first a red-back bite feels like a bee sting and is not too painful. However, after a few minutes, pain can spread to the rest of the body. Victims often suffer from sweating, weakness of muscles and fever – some victims cannot move at all.

Real life story

In 2001, Darren Meehan from Alice Springs, Australia was bitten by a red-back spider more than 20 times on the bottom. The 25-year-old needed 16 doses of antivenin to survive. Darren thinks he trapped the spider in his jeans during a visit to an outside toilet.

Scary Sydney funnelwebs

Sydney funnelwebs are found in the areas around Sydney, Australia. They are one of Australia's most poisonous and aggressive spiders.

If a Sydney funnelweb feels threatened, it will stand up and show its sharp fangs to scare away the danger.

Vital statistics

Sydney funnelwebs are usually 2.5–3 centimetres long. Their legs can be up to 4 centimetres long. They have black heads and their abdomens are a dark plum colour. These dangerous spiders have huge, strong fangs. The fangs are strong enough to bite right through a human fingernail!

How they kill

Sydney funnelwebs spin their funnel-shaped webs in damp, dark places — usually under logs and rocks. Webs have even been found in shoes! Like hobo spiders, funnelwebs spin long trip-lines around their webs to trap their prey. When prey is caught in the trip-lines, the spiders rush out and kill it with their deadly fangs. They hang on to their prey and bite again and again. Once the prey is dead, they take it back to their web to eat it.

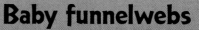

Fact!

Funnelweb venom can be fatal for humans and apes, but it has little effect on other mammals.

Encounters with people

As funnelwebs are found in cities and towns, they often come into contact with people. Unlike other spiders, the males are more dangerous than the females. When they bite, they inject huge amounts of venom. The bite can cause numbness in the mouth, vomiting, and stomach pains. If an antivenin is not given, victims can die in 15 minutes.

Baby funnelwebs

Female Sydney funnelwebs spin a silky, cushion-shaped egg sac. They can lay more than 100 eggs inside each sac. The females guard the egg sac for three weeks, until the baby funnelwebs hatch.

Key words

Abdomen
The lower part of a spider's body.

Aggressive
A spider that is dangerous and may attack for no reason is aggressive.

Antivenin
The medicine given to fight the effect of venom – it is usually made from spiders' venom.

Burrow
A hole dug by an animal.

Conservation
Keeping the natural environment in a good state. For example, protecting animals and their habitats.

Digestive juices
The chemicals that spiders make to help them break down their food so that they can eat it.

Dose
A specific amount of medicine that must be taken.

Endangered species
A group of living things in danger of dying out completely.

Fangs
A spider's long hollow teeth. Spiders use their fangs to inject deadly venom and to attack or stab their prey.

Fatal
When something ends in death.

Flesh-eating disease
A disease where a person's flesh rots away in open sores called ulcers.

Funnel-shaped
A tube that that starts out wide and has a narrow end is funnel-shaped. For example, an ice-cream cone.

Habitat
The place where particular plants and animals live.

Harmless
Not dangerous or harmful.

Hourglass
An instrument that measures time. It looks like a traditional egg timer.

Leg-span
The distance from one end of a spider's longest leg to the other.

Mammals
Animals with fur or hair that feed their young with their own milk. Most mammals give birth to live young.

Moult
To shed skin.

Nocturnal
A spider that is active at night is nocturnal.

Pesticides
Dangerous substances or chemicals that are used to kill spiders and other harmful bugs.

Reptiles
The cold-blooded animals that have backbones and scaly skin.

Scavenger
An animal that feeds off other dead animals.

Species
A group of living things that can breed with one another.

Tropical
To do with the area near to the tropics that has a warm climate.

Venom
Poison. A spider with venom in its fangs is called venomous.

Weblinks

http://classroomclipart.com/cgi-bin/kids/imageFolio.cgi?direct=Animals/Spiders
Great photographs of spiders to use in classroom activities.

http://www.enchantedlearning.com/subjects/arachnids/Arachnidprintouts.shtml
Lots of interesting facts about spiders plus activities to print out.

http://www.giantspiders.com/
Find out more about the biggest spiders in the world.

www.amonline.net.au/spiders/
Everything you ever wanted to know about Australia's spiders.

http://www.arachnology.be/pages/Kids.html
Lots of information on spiders.

www.dltk-kids.com/crafts/insects/crafts-spiders.htm
Fun spider arts and crafts things to do.

Note to parents:
Every effort has been made by the publishers to ensure that the websites in this book are suitable for children, that they are of the highest educational value, and that they contain no inappropriate or offensive material. However, due to the nature of the Internet, it is impossible to guarantee that the contents of these sites will not be altered. We strongly advise that Internet access is supervised by a responsible adult.

Index